PROCRASTINATION

Overcome the Bad Habits of Procrastination and Laziness and Become More Productive

BOOK DESCRIPTION

There is nothing that depresses productivity and stunts personal development more than procrastination. Yet, procrastination creeps slowly and meekly into our lives through the very same shortcuts that we engaged to allow us comfort and convenience - bad habits.

This book, "Procrastination: Overcome the bad habits of procrastination and laziness and become more productive" has been specifically written to enable you kick out procrastination, regain your productivity and achieve your full potential.

The book starts by introducing you to what procrastination really is and provides you with telling signs of procrastination, some of them often hidden and uneasy to detect. It further cautions you on the pitfalls you are likely to fall into should you not be careful and the negative effects of procrastination.

Most people never realize that they are procrastinators. Never assume you are not one unless you prove it. A simple, yet powerful **self-diagnosis procrastination test** kit has been devised for you. Should you find yourself not a procrastinator, that would be great for you. However, it does not end there. You can use the same kit to help your family, friends and loved ones who could be suffering from procrastination without knowing it. Discovery is the best way to finding a lasting solution.

The best way to confront a disease it to go beyond its symptoms and attack its root causes. Some of the root causes may be common to all procrastinators while others could be unique to each procrastinator. Nonetheless, this book provides all likely causes of procrastination so that you can review and evaluate your very own condition and determine the most likely causes of your procrastination.

Once you determine the root causes of your procrastination, the next obvious step is to heal it. This book provides you with the most elaborate, powerful and effective ways to overcome procrastination.

Procrastination is an aggregate collection of bad habits which results into you delaying your decision or action without prudence. Like all bad habits, the best way to overcome procrastination is to engender good daily habits that will help you to prevent, avoid or nullify bad habits. Powerful and effective daily habits have been prescribed, which, if you diligently employ, will permanently keep off procrastination from your life.

Lastly, but not least, every endeavor has a reward. The rewards of overcoming procrastination are immense and unlimited. Yet, this book provides you with the most obvious rewards that you will gain in the most prominent facets of your life - health, relationships and money.

Enjoy reading.

GIFT INCLUDED

If you are an entrepreneur, an aspiring entrepreneur, someone who is trying to create additional income stream, or even someone who just loves self improvement books; then you need to read my recommendations for top 10 business books ever. These are book that I have read that have changed my life for the better.

Top 10 Business Books

ABOUT THE AUTHOR

George Pain is an entrepreneur, author and business consultant. He specializes in setting up online businesses from scratch, investment income strategies and global mobility solutions. He has built several businesses from the ground up, and is excited to share his knowledge with readers. Here is a list of his books.

Books of George Pain

DISCLAIMER

Copyright © 2017

All Rights Reserved

No part of this book can be transmitted or reproduced in any form including print, electronic, photocopying, scanning, mechanical or recording without prior written permission from the author.

While the author has taken the utmost effort to ensure the accuracy of the written content, all readers are advised to follow information mentioned herein at their own risk. The author cannot be held responsible for any personal or commercial damage caused by information. All readers are encouraged to seek professional advice when needed.

CONTENTS

PROCRASTINATION 1

BOOK DESCRIPTION 2

GIFT INCLUDED 5

ABOUT THE AUTHOR 6

DISCLAIMER 7

CONTENTS 8

INTRODUCTION 9

WHAT IS PROCRASTINATION? 10

TAKE THE PROCRASTINATION QUIZ 13

MOST COMMON REASONS FOR PROCRASTINATION 20

WAYS TO OVERCOME PROCRASTINATION 31

DAILY HABITS TO OVERCOME PROCRASTINATION 57

IMPROVE YOUR HEALTH, RELATINSHIPS AND MONEY 64

CONCLUSION 76

INTRODUCTION

Sometimes we prudently delay making decisions. This is absolutely noble. However, many a time, we find ourselves delaying decisions and then, later on we start asking "why did I really not do it on time?"

Whenever you find yourself persistently not being able to justify as to why you delay making decisions or taking actions, know that you are suffering from procrastination.

Procrastination has been commonly accused of being the thief of time. As you shall find out later in this book, procrastination is a much bigger thief. Procrastination not only steals your time, but also your health, wealth, money, satisfaction, joy and happiness.

Luckily, you don't have to suffer from ravages of procrastination. This book, "Procrastination: overcome the bad habits of procrastination and laziness and become more productive", has been specifically written just for you. The intent of this book is to liberate you from procrastination, help you stay away from laziness and regain your productivity, health, wealth and happiness. Keep reading!

WHAT IS PROCRASTINATION?

Millions of opportunities are thrown to the trashcan and billions of labor hours lost across the world. There is no greater thief of time, labor and opportunity than procrastination.

The world is full of people who remain mediocre simply because the vagaries of procrastination have ensured that they never achieve their full potential. You have to liberate yourself from this silent thief ravaging your chances to grab every other opportunity to prosper. This book is all you need to transform yourself into that fortress which the waves of procrastination would hit and crumble. This book is the rock to build your fortress.

What is procrastination?

Procrastination is a defective attitude encrusted into your subconscious mind to bring forth a self-defeating habitual pattern of delays. It also involves avoiding taking bold steps towards new opportunities.

To be able to determine as to whether you are a victim of procrastination or not, you need to master telling signs of procrastination so that you can carry out self-diagnosis, positively identify it and take appropriate remedial actions provided later within this book.

What are the key symptoms of procrastination?

Procrastination is a condition characterized by the following symptoms;

- Inability to make quick decisions
- Inordinate delay in taking appropriate action
- Inertia in taking advantage of opportunities
- Willful surrender to the passage of time
- Lack of willpower
- Low energy

What are the negative effects of procrastination?

Opportunities are always the stepping stones covered by the carpet of challenge. Thus, if you fear the carpet, then, you won't climb onto the stairs of success, prosperity and happiness.

Opportunities hardly knock twice. You fail to open up for one; it dissolves into the passing clouds forever. More often than not, opportunities disguise themselves as 'problems'. However, whether these are genuinely 'problems' or 'challenges' solely depend on your attitude. It is a question akin to your perception as to whether the glass is half-full or half-empty. "Half-full" could mean a challenge, while "half-empty" could mean a problem. Yet, it is still one and the same state of things, only differentiated by your attitude.

Most of procrastinators see problems rather than challenges. They have that avoidance attitude wired into their mindset. Naturally, we are predisposed to avoid problems. So, when we erroneously see a challenge as a 'problem' then, we are likely to avoid them.

There are unlimited negative effects of procrastination depending on each opportunity lost. Nonetheless, the following are the generally known negative effects of procrastination;

- Mediocrity
- Lack of growth and progress
- Poor performance
- Stress

ARE YOU A PROCRASTINATOR? – TAKE THE PROCRASTINATION QUIZ

In the previous section, we have seen the causes and symptoms of procrastination. However, there are those times when prudence and procrastination can be confused. Prudence is about taking precautions so as to avoid unnecessary risks, which, in essence, could at times lead to informed delay. On the other hand, procrastination is delaying an action not based on precautionary steps or informed delay but simply inertia.

To be able to make an informed diagnosis of your status, then, you need to carry out procrastination quiz (test).

YOUR SIMPLE SELF-DIAGNOSIS PROCRASTINATION TEST

The following simple quiz can help you detect as to whether you are a procrastinator or not;

[Mark the right Choice]

1. Due to postponing actions, I often find myself overwhelmed by lack of time near deadlines
    a) Yes
    b) Occasionally
    c) No
2. I find it torturous to start off working on things that I find unpleasant
    a) Yes
    b) Occasionally
    c) No
3. I am consciously struggling to do things right now, but I always find myself still doing them late
    a) Yes
    b) Occasionally
    c) No
4. I am predisposed to postponing action even though I am fully aware of its absolute importance
    a) Yes
    b) Occasionally
    c) No
5. "Better late than now" has been my unconscious motto
    a) Yes
    b) Occasionally
    c) No

6. I postpone things that I find difficult to do, until later
    a) Yes
    b) Occasionally
    c) No
7. While carrying out an important task, I always find myself being overwhelmed by razing thoughts pulling me away into indulgence of unnecessary and non-urgent endeavors such as chatting on social media, playing games, and watching cartoons.
    a) Yes
    b) Occasionally
    c) No
8. I prefer drawing a TO DO List, yet I often fail to implement it conclusively
    a) Yes
    b) Occasionally
    c) No
9. I am more inclined to wait until deadline is near
    a) Yes
    b) Occasionally
    c) No

10. **Most of the time, I pay my bills late**
    a) Yes
    b) Occasionally
    c) No

YOUR TEST RESULTS INTERPRETATION:

1. If your choice is **(a)** in all or almost all of the above, then you are a habitual procrastinator.
2. If your choice is **(b)** in all or almost all of the above, then you occasionally procrastinate, though, it is not yet habitual
3. If your choice is **(c)** in all or almost all of the above, then, you have no reason to worry for you are not a procrastinator.

WHAT SHOULD I DO NEXT?

Whatever the outcome of your result, simply don't procrastinate! Do something.

If you are a procrastinator (habitual or not), help yourself by learning;

1. The most common reasons for procrastination
2. Ways to overcome procrastination
3. Daily habits to prevent procrastination

4. How overcoming procrastination will improve your health, relationship and money

If you are not a procrastinator, you have to understand that **nobody is born a procrastinator**. Thus, **procrastination is acquired**, at times, unknowingly. Hence, you too, need to learn how to avoid the common pitfalls that cause procrastination. More important than anything else, learn;

1. The most common reasons for procrastination
2. Ways to overcome procrastination
3. Daily habits to prevent procrastination
4. How overcoming procrastination will improve your health, relationship and money

So that, you can not only save yourself from becoming a victim of procrastination but also help others who are already suffering from procrastination.

When you suspect that your friend, family member, colleague or loved one is suffering from procrastination, share with him/her the knowledge provided in this book and help him/her carry out the above self-diagnosis procrastination test in an honest and unbiased manner.

A Short message from the Author:

Hey, are you enjoying the book? I'd love to hear your thoughts!

Many readers do not know how hard reviews are to come by, and how much they help an author.

I would be incredibly thankful if you could take just 60 seconds to write a brief review on Amazon, even if it's just a few sentences!

Please head to the product page, and leave a review as shown below.

Customer Reviews

★★★★★ 2

5.0 out of 5 stars ▼

5 star		100%
4 star		0%
3 star		0%
2 star		0%

Share your thoughts with other

Write a customer review

Thank you for taking the time to share your thoughts!

Your review will genuinely make a difference for me and help gain exposure for my work.

MOST COMMON REASONS FOR PROCRASTINATION

Procrastination is a psychological condition with deeply rooted causes. The following are some of the main causes of procrastination;

- Fear
- Poor attitude
- Bad habits
- Low self-esteem
- Defective mindset

Procrastination being a condition, it simply means that it is an aggregate symptom rather than a disease. It warns you that you are suffering from certain disease(s) that you ought to confront. Thus, while addressing procrastination, we must go further than 'what it is' and address 'what it is telling us' about.

To be able to gain a better understanding of the nature of procrastination, we need to dwell a bit deeper into each of the above causes.

Fear

Fear is a kind of feeling experienced by one's perception of threat or danger which causes bodily changes that result into change in behavior such as frowning, hiding or fleeing from the perceived traumatic event.

This perception is based on what is recorded in the unconscious mind and accessed, read and interpreted by the subconscious mind.

Types of fear

Fear is classified into two broad categories;

Rational fear – This is fear that is beneficial. It is kind of fear that saves you from danger such as a wild animal, oncoming car that is out of control, a flooding river that has broken its banks, a swarm of bees, violent storm, among other visible traumatic events. This fear is like an alarm that seeks to protect you from harm and is healthy for every human being and animals as essential for their very own security and survival. It is this rational fear that calls for PRUDENCE.

Irrational fear (phobia) – This is basically a psychological fear. It is not based on physical threat. It is based on conditioning of the mind. It is this irrational fear that causes PROCRASTINATION.

Phobia

There are three main types of phobia;

1. **Simple (Specific) phobias** – There are many other specific kind of fears each towards a specific object. There are more than hundred of them. For example, fear of dogs, cats, spiders, cars, etc. They usually occur during childhood and often disappear when one attains adulthood.
2. **Complex phobias** – These are phobias that have serious disabling or disruptive consequences on life. They tend to develop when one is already an adult. The two common kinds of these phobias are;
   - **Social phobia** – This is extreme fear of social situations which leads one to isolate himself from others. It is commonly referred to social anxiety disorder.
   - **Agoraphobia** – This is fear of open spaces. One feels helpless while in open space and thus would like to stay indoors. This may have been induced by traumatic event such as storm, falling trees, bombs being dropped in war zones, etc.

There are many more complex phobias.

Why does phobia come about?

There are several reasons as to why phobia comes about. The following are the key;

- Specific trauma. For example, if you were hit by flying or falling objects maybe due to storm or bombs, you are more likely develop fear of open spaces. If you were terribly scolded as a child in a social place, you may develop social trauma.
- Learned responses. Some phobias are transmitted from parents or people of influence.
- Response to panic or physical fear. If people responded to you negatively about a certain panic, e.g. of screaming because you were absent-minded while crossing the road not realizing that a car was getting closer, you are more likely develop a phobia of crossing the roads.
- Long-term stress. Stress causes anxiety and to the extreme, depression. If you have been a victim of these, then, you are more likely going to develop a phobia for fearing such kind of situation repeating.
- Genetics. Genetics play a big role in phobias. Some people are genetically more prone to phobias than others.

How fear get ingrained in your unconscious mind

Whenever a certain traumatic event occurs, its records are stored in the unconscious mind which exists in the Amygdala part of the brain.

In this storage, all details surrounding the traumatic event are recorded including the sight, sound, odor, time, weather, etc.

When a combination of some or most of these stored details occur, the brain short-circuits the rational pathway of thought and reacts immediately to Amygdala thus triggering the fight or flight mechanism which causes one to either fight the perceived danger or flee it. PROCRASTINATION IS MORE ABOUT FLIGHT.

This, it happens frequently upon a habitual trigger of fear (provided the cues come in the form of sight, sound, odor and other such are details that characterize the initial traumatic event).

Because these cues were associated with a previous danger or trauma, every time they occur the brain interprets them as predictors of threat. This results in chronic fear if the cues happen more often.

Negative effects of fear

Fear can cause:

- Disorientation of one's perception – Fear can cause disorientation in the way one perceives (interprets incoming signals through the five senses) something, thus subjecting the brain to misinterpretation of the input and resulting in an erroneous response.
- Stifled thoughts and actions – Fear can cause people to block their mental process of thinking. There are those who believe it is a taboo to think about certain things such as the nature of God, sex, money and such other topics.
- Destructive habits – Fear can create destructive habits such as drug addiction and substance abuse.
- Lack of peace and contentment – Living in constant fear deprives one of sleep, rest, peace and contentment.
- Negative behavior – Since fear can breed either fight or flight, some people may develop social anxiety disorder or aggressiveness whenever certain cues take place, e.g. when someone laughs, when someone stares at them, etc.
- Cardiovascular damage – Fear triggers release of hormones that increase the level of adrenaline for the flight mode. This increase the heart's pump rate. If this becomes frequent or chronic or so acute, some blood vessels, mostly in the heart become damaged. This may result into heart attack.
- Gastrointestinal problems – ulcers and irritable bowel symptom are some of the common side effects of phobia.
- Decreased fertility – Phobia causes decline in libido. This decreases generation of hormones responsible for

triggering sperm and ova generation. The end result is declined interest in sex.
- Neurological damage – Persistent or chronic fear can cause damage to the hippocampus, a part of the brain responsible for memory, emotions and autonomic nervous system. This damage may trigger early onset of Alzheimer's disease.
- Clinical depression – Chronic stress and anxiety due to fear may induce clinical depression
- Accelerated ageing – Accelerated ageing may become the consequence of some of the mentioned negative effects. It is like the brain communicates to the body to exit life at shorter duration than expected.
- Premature death – Premature death can be triggered by a combination of the mentioned negative effects.

You can easily see from these side effects that psychological fear is the greatest enemy that rests hidden in your subconscious mind.

Negative psychological effects of fear

It is fear that makes people entertain negative beliefs. It is fear that makes people lose self-esteem. It is fear that makes people surrender to that which makes them not exploit their full potential.

Fear makes people stick to their comfort zone not wanting to risk adventure. Superstitions, taboos, traditions are all products of fear. Fear of change and adventure.

Fear causes people to embrace and stick to destructive habits such as procrastination, escapism, scapegoating, and seeking every excuse to fail.

How to overcome phobia (psychological fear)

Both rational and irrational fears are as a result of mindset. A program etched in your unconscious mind and which is accessed and interpreted by your subconscious mind instructs your brain on what to do whenever your consciousness detects the occurrence of a certain traumatic event.

Thus, the best way to overcome phobia is reset your mindset. That is, reprogram your mindset. It is akin to flashing out old memories.

Phobia overcoming techniques

There are various psychotherapy techniques that you can employ to overcome your fears. These include;

- Mindfulness Meditation
- Neuro-Linguistic Programming (NLP)
- Positive Thinking
- Creative visualizations
- Power posing

These are general psychological tools and techniques that you can easily customize to fight against other psychological conditions such as procrastination and its various other causes such as poor attitude, bad habits, low self-esteem and defective mindset.

Poor attitude

As we shall see later in the next section, an attitude is simply a mental predisposition. It is how your mindset is wired to perceive and respond to certain stimuli.

Bad habits

Fear and/or poor attitude greatly contribute to bad habits. Whenever there are bad habits, poor attitude will never miss. Fear will hardly miss.

As we shall also see later in the next section, bad habits are simply those habits that prevent you from achieving the best of your being.

Low self-esteem

Poor attitude and bad habits are products of low self-esteem. Fear could be a cause of low self-esteem. Fear can also be a product of low self-esteem. However, the predominant cause of low self-esteem is the negative self-image that you have wired into your defective mindset.

This negative self-image is caused by past negative experiences that you went through. For example, traumatic childhood abuse by parents or caregivers, abuse by teachers, bullying by your peers, and mistreatment by your bosses at work, among others.

These past experiences resulted into you feeling a lesser being than you are. They created that impression that you are not worthy before others.

Low self-esteem has been predominant cause of bad habits such as alcohol and drug abuse, child molestation, rapes, aggressiveness, emotional outbursts, poor relationships, etc.

We shall discuss more issues related to self esteem in the next section.

Defective mindset

A defective mindset is a mindset that binds you into an endless web of misery. Taking computer analogy, it is a mindset that is poorly programmed and thus runs like a 'virus', 'worm' or 'enemy bots' within your brain.

We shall delve further on mindset and how to detect and correct defective mindset in our next Section.

WAYS TO OVERCOME PROCRASTINATION

To overcome procrastination, it is extremely important that you first isolate the disease from its symptoms. When you treat the disease, the symptoms will naturally die. However, when you focus on treating the symptoms, you will get temporary relief while the disease remains uncured.

We have already discussed the causes and symptoms of procrastination in the first and second Sections. In this Section we want to dwell on dealing with the disease itself.

The following are key steps to overcoming procrastination;

1. Know what to do
2. Device action plan
3. Sharpen your resolve (tools and techniques)
4. Work on your mindset
5. Work on your habit

Know what to do

Knowledge is power. In the first section, we started off by embarking on knowledge of what procrastination is. In the second section, we devised a simple yet powerful self-diagnosis procrastination test. In the third section we explored most common reasons for procrastination.

Right now, let's explore knowing what to do in order to overcome procrastination. Previously, we found out that the most fertile contributor to procrastination is lack of action plan. When you have no action plan you are more likely than not to sway away into procrastination. Thus, the first action is drawing the action plan itself.

The second important thing to do is to sharpen your resolve. It is lack of determination and self-discipline that denies you focus on your goal. Thus, to be able to discipline yourself to focus on your goal, you must sharpen your resolve.

You must have realized that, sharpening your resolve is mind-driven. Thus, you must work on your mind in order to succeed in sharpening your resolve. Your mind is the ground in which the tree of procrastination has its deep roots and derives its rich nutrients.

As we have seen in our first Section, procrastination is a habit. Like all other bad habits, procrastination begins in the mind. That's also the very place it must begin to be fought.

Sharpen your resolve

Sharpening your resolve requires you to regain your lost Willpower. Willpower is that innate ability to overcome inherent inertia. The greatest reason why procrastination happens is inertia. Due to all the other reasons we have discussed and shall continue to discuss, inertia brings that lazy reluctance to take action. You want to stand up but something seems to hook you onto the seat; you want to wake up but something seems to pin you down on the bed; you want to walk out but something seems to glue you onto the sofa. You want to leave chatting on social media but something still nags and seems to shout 'wait for my next post!'; You seem to be arrested into a perpetual vicious cycle of waiting; You snap out from one cycle of waiting into the next cycle of waiting.

Your endless cycle of waiting cranks your willpower stamina making it impotent when needed.

Willpower is that force that urges you to actualize your will. It keeps you focused on asserting your determined will regardless of the swaying from others, be it persuasive or coercive.

Key attributes of willpower are;

- Ability to postpone instant gratification
- Ability to overcome bursts of short-term emotional temptations in order to achieve long-term goals
- Ability to override destructive thoughts and impulses
- Self-control

Lack of willpower is due to many mind problems. However, the following are the most prominent causes of lack of willpower which you must confront in order to sharpen your resolve to end procrastination;

- Scarcity – Perpetual scarcity makes it easy for people to lose their willpower. For example, those who wish to have a balanced diet may give up on their willpower if inadequate supplies of fruits and vegetables become perpetual.

- Money troubles - Studies found out that money troubles have strong negative psychological effect on the poor. Money troubles impair their thought-process as they slowly adapt to conditions that requires less willpower to overcome. For example, it is a bad habit to pick from dumpsites, but money troubles may cause the poor to do that not because they don't know it is a bad habit, but their willpower has been lowered by money troubles.

- Constant decision-making – When people encounter many scenarios that require quick and constant decision-making, their mind gets worked-up and soon their willpower to continue making more decisions gets impaired.

- Stress – Stress is as a result of overworked mental energy. Willpower consumes energy. Thus, when you are stressed, there is less energy available to your willpower.

Device action plan

An action plan is simply an executable plan. It is a plan that you have to carry out in order to achieve your goal. In this case, your goal is A LIFE FREE FROM PROCRASTINATION. Though, as we shall see later, this is still not yet the SMARTEST goal. But, for the time being, let it hold.

Life without a plan is the most chaotic of all lives that could ever be lived. You need not sweat out having complex plans that make your life harder than it ought to be or even much worse without it. To achieve unique and exceptional personal development, the goal of your life must be to make it EASIER.

An EASIER plan of action. This encompasses six critical components;

1. Envision
2. Assess
3. Strategize
4. Implement
5. Evaluate
6. Reward/Reprimand

Thus, EASIER is an acronym that stands for **E**nvision, **A**ssess, **S**trategize, **I**mplement, **E**valuate, and **R**eward.

Envision

To envision is to dream and visualize your dream. Once you have visualized your dreams, it becomes easy to idealize them. In envisioning, place yourself into that future you dream of and see your being in it.

Thus, to envision encompasses three critical steps;

- Dream
- Idealize
- Visualize
- Engender

Dream

Dreaming is the nursery from which ideas germinate. The seeds for these ideas are the imaginations. To dream is simply to tantalize imagination, to entertain it and help it grow. With a dream big enough to be formidable, the next step is to idealize it.

Idealize

To idealize your dream is to map it out with clear points of reference. It is to refine and define it into a form that can be visualized.

Visualize

This is the core of envisioning. It is casting the map work of your dream into a grander scale with a clear perspective that can be easily assessed and actualized through strategy.

Visualizing is the process of creating a VISION. A vision is a state of being once your MISSION is accomplished and your GOAL achieved.

In this case, the vision is A HEALTHY AND WEALTHY LIFE RICHLY ENDOWED BY LOVING RELATIONSHIPS

Engender

To engender is to take ownership of your vision; to place it at the core of your heart; to humanize it; to make it capable of passion and effort. It is indeed to embrace your vision.

Assess

To assess is to make an analysis of what you envision, your capabilities required to achieve your vision, the ideas that come out of your mind in line with your vision, the prevailing circumstances and situations.

The most significant tool for carrying out self-assessment or of that situation at hand is SWOT analysis.

SWOT analysis encompasses the following five elements;

- Your **S**trengths
- Your **W**eaknesses
- Your **O**pportunities
- Your **T**hreats

Procrastination requires a deep SWOT analysis so that you can be able to efficiently and effectively confront it.

SWOT your core inner variables

When you are making a SWOT analysis of yourself, the core variable that you would consider are those that form your inner being where your dreams, idealizations, visions and engenders are formed: Where their energizing power derive their source – right within your inner self.

The following are those core inner variables that you must SWOT about;

- Attitudes
- Habits
- Beliefs
- Fears

These are the very same variables that play a greater role in creating or ending procrastination.

Attitudes

An attitude is a learned tendency to evaluate matters in a certain manner. Such matters include people, objects, events, issues, etc.

Attitudes have three critical components;

- **Emotional component** – How matters under evaluation make you feel.
- **Cognitive component** – Your thoughts and beliefs about matters at hand.
- **Behavioral component** – How your perception/evaluation influences your behavior.

Habits

A habit is a repetitive pattern of arriving at a certain outcome. This pattern could be a pattern of thoughts, actions of reactions.

Beliefs

A belief is a mental representation of an attitude towards the likelihood of a state being (or an outcome turning out) in a certain way.

Your mindset – the home to your inner variables

Your mindset is where your inner variables reside. You wholly depend on your mindset. Your mindset is the blueprint of your life.

Carry out a Self SWOT Analysis

SWOT analysis is a tool that helps you to evaluate your strengths, weaknesses, opportunities and threats.

Strengths

Strength is the power or advantage you have in carrying out a given responsibility. The following are some of the key elements of your strengths;

- **Positive attitudes.** These are the attitudes that help you get the best out of your life. List them down so that you can able to see how best to employ them in your strategy. Some of the positive attitudes could include; being

optimistic, seeing the best in others, not being bogged down by failures, etc.
- **Good habits**. These are those habits that have enabled you to achieve success in your endeavors. Such habits include; waking up early, being punctual, smiling at guests and strangers, greeting people, making yourself available at others service, etc.
- **Ownership**. This refers to being able to take responsibility and be accountable to your deeds, be they positive or negative. When you accept your fault without resorting to excuses that means you own your responsibility.
- **Assertiveness**. This refers to being in charge of and influencing other people's decisions in a way that helps you achieve your objectives. Assertiveness is about being polite and bold. It should be free from aggression and arrogance.

Your strengths are your assets at your disposal which you can employ to overcome procrastination. Work to enhance them and utilize them well.

Weaknesses

Weaknesses are those elements of your being that draws you back from achieving the best of your endeavors. Some of these elements include;

- **Fear**. This is a weakness that is characterized by worrying, lack of confidence, loss of self-will and declined willpower.
- **Negative attitudes**. Negative attitudes are those attitudes that prevent you from achieving your highest potential. They include; being persistently pessimistic, looking down upon others, stereotyping, etc.
- **Negative beliefs** – These are believes that hold you back. They are stumbling blocks that stop you from making certain positive endeavors in your life. Some of these negative beliefs include; believing that you can't make it in life, believing that no one loves you, believing that everyone is against you, believing that you have been bewitched or cursed and as such nothing of your endeavors can succeed, etc.
- **Bad habits**. Bad habits are those habits that don't help you to be a better person. They negate your positive endeavors. Bad habits include waking up late, addiction, obsession, chewing in office, poor hygiene, insulting others, gossiping, etc.

You need to keep a watch on your weaknesses. Do your best to eliminate them so that you optimize on your success and make your life easier.

Opportunities

Life presents an abundant supply of opportunities. Opportunities flow like winds over the oceans. You are the captain of your boat. To take advantage of these opportunities depends on how you manage your sails. You have so many opportunities at your disposal to end procrastination.

Some of the common opportunities available to you are;

- **Room for change**. Change is the only constant that isn't constant. There will be always limitless room for change for so long as you are willing to change.
- **Reward for change**. Every change endeavor has its own reward. Some of may seem apparent while others may not. The good thing is that change will always have its own reward for so long as you are ready to embrace it.
- **Chances for advancement**. Be it in personal development, career, or otherwise, there will always be plenty of chances for advancement. Some of the chances include a whole host of sacrifices. It is up to you to find

ways to lower the cost of sacrifices in order for you to optimize on the likely benefits.

Opportunities are the fruits that are within your reach. Seize them. Take advantage of them. The more you utilize your opportunities the greater is your reward in your success endeavor.

Threats

Threats are those imminent risks that have the likelihood of derailing your given endeavor. Some inherent threats embedded in you that can derail your endeavors include;

- **Inability to overcome negative self-image.** Negative self image is that image that you've have created that portrays you as less than who you truly are. They are image created from past negative experiences. They have resulted from poor childhood upbringing (such abuses by parents, teachers and other caregivers), poor grades in school, psychological trauma (such as from loss of a loved one, violent political suppression, etc), among others. Negative self-image points to every opportunity as a problem and likely adversity.
- **Inability to overcome low self-esteem.** Low self-esteem is the negative behavioral outcome of negative self image. You feel less than who you ought to be. You don't trust yourself to do certain things in life. Low self-esteem

treats every opportunity as an insurmountable task that you can't dare or succeed in carrying out.
- **Inability to have confidence**. Lack of self-confidence is the consequence of low self-esteem. Lack of confidence breeds fear. You feel you are not strong enough to take the challenge required to exploit a given opportunity.

Threats, like weaknesses, serve to disadvantage you. Threats are the imminent dangers that can prevent you from achieving your goals. You have to work on them in order to ensure successful achievement of your goal.

Strategize

To strategize is to set an action plan, or simply, plan of action to actualize your vision. This action plan must encompass your mission, goals, objectives, tasks, targets and tactics.

In strategizing, you have to create a Planning Mindset that will help you set SMARTEST goals, break (decompose) your goals into functional domains (e.g. tasks, departments, milestones, etc) for easier handling. With SMARTEST goals established, the next thing is to implement your strategy.

- Create a planning mindset
- Set SMARTEST goals

- Decompose goals into functional domains
- Set manageable targets

Creating a planning mindset

Your mindset is the garden where your ideas grow and mature into plans. How healthy your ideas become depends solely on how you tend to this garden. Make it fertile and your ideas will become healthy and prosperous. You achieve this by working on your mindset.

Work on your mindset

A mindset is a set of beliefs, assumptions and thoughts that make up one's mental attitude, habit, inclination or disposition which predetermines a person's perceptions and responses to situations, circumstances and events.

Why is mindset such important?

Mindset is important because it is the point of reference with which you perceive and respond to events, circumstances and situation. How you perceive things depends on your mindset. That's why many experts say that 'you see things as you are' and not necessarily as they are. This 'you are' is your mindset.

Mindset is the fertile ground upon which the seed of vision grows. How healthy and great your vision becomes solely depend on your mindset. A defective mindset will definitely yield a defective vision. A fixed mindset will yield a fixed vision. And thus, a transformational (growth) mindset will yield a transformational vision.

Fixed vs. Growth Mindset

There are two main types of mindset – fixed and growth mindset.

A fixed mindset is that which holds that one's basic qualities such as intelligence and talents are fixed traits such that nothing can be done to improve them.

A growth mindset is that which holds that one's basic qualities such as intelligence and talents can be developed through dedication and hard work and they are just a stepping stone to greater things.

Why a planning mindset is a growth mindset

Plans are never fixed. The best plan is that plan that is flexible enough to grow with changing circumstances, situations and events. A fixed plan most likely fails since all plans are about unpredictable future which may not necessarily unravel as one predicted.

Thus, a planning mindset has to be a growth mindset if these plans have to really been made with success in mind.

Vision: the place where your goal post ought to reside

Vision is the big picture of how things ought to be. Vision is what you would like to see once you have accomplished your mission and achieved your goal.

Why have a Vision?

The following are the key purposes of a Vision.
1. It inspires you to take appropriate action
2. It helps you to communicate effectively with an inner compulsion
3. It helps you to marshal resources and rally people towards a common purpose
4. It empowers everyone who is inspired by it to achieve it.

The three essential qualities of your vision

A. Core Ideology

A core ideology is that set of ideals that inspire you to marshal your mind, heart and sinew towards achieving a certain goal

There are two key elements;

1. **Core values** – These are the overriding principles that guide your life.
2. **Core purpose** – this is the key reason why you think you live.

B. Envisioned future

This is the picture of what you perceive to be your future.

C. Your attitude

This is your mental predisposition.

How to create a vision

1. Establish your core ideology.
2. Break it down into distinct core values. Values are those essential qualities/principles that you believe are important in the way you live and work.
3. Blend your mission and core values to come up with an inspiring core purpose.

How to write down a Vision Statement

A Vision Statement is the most important statement of you. It is the foundation of all other statements that will ever come out of you about you.

The following are key steps to writing down a Vision Statement;

1. Set the time frame
2. Write the first draft
3. Seek feedback over your draft
4. Rewrite your draft based on the feedback obtained
5. Share your vision

In our case, our vision is: A HEALTHY AND WEALTHY LIFE RICHLY ENDOWED BY LOVING RELATIONSHIPS

Mission: the key reason why you want to achieve your goals

A mission is the 'raison detre' or reason for existence of your organization.

How to create a Mission

The sole purpose of a mission is to achieve a given set of goals.

Key qualities of a good Mission Statement

A good mission statement should;

1. Describe what your being is
2. Describe what your being seeks to do and why it seeks to do it
3. Be clear and concise
4. Be outcome-oriented
5. Be considerate of your key stakeholders – your family, your partner(s), friends, your colleagues, your employer, etc.

Salient questions that you must answer in your Mission

1. Who am I?
2. Why did I about?
3. What do I intent to do?
4. For whom do I intent do it?
5. Why do I intent to serve my being the way I propose?

6. What distinguishes my vision from my current state?
7. How do I get my key stakeholders to understand my mission?

How to develop your Mission Statement

1. Develop a compelling call
2. Clarify your goal
3. Capture and inspire your imagination
4. Manifest your core competencies
5. Motivate and inspire your commitment
6. Be realistic
7. Be specific, short, sharp and memorable

How to write down a Mission Statement

The steps for writing a Mission Statement are the same as those for writing a Vision Statement.

In our case, you can state your Mission as;

TO END PROCRASTINATION SO THAT I CAN ENJOY A HEALTHY AND WEALTHY LIFE RICHLY ENDOWED BY LOVING RELATIONSHIPS

Setting SMARTEST goals

Without a goal there is no achievement. It is like a body running without a head – such movement will be random, aimless and short-lived. A goal is an end that you pursue. It is a specific accomplishment that you desire at the end of your endeavor. It is the ultimate prize that you want to get out of your endeavor.

Why have a goal?

There are many benefits that accrue to your endeavor if it has a goal. A goal enables you to;

1. Have a direction
2. Be focused
3. Plan on what you can do to achieve your ultimate end
4. Be disciplined
5. Be able to measure your success

How do you create the SMARTEST goal?

A goal that will enable you to be able to achieve the best of your endeavor is a one which is the SMARTEST of all goals.

For example, if you are in debt and you would like to get out of it;

> *Free myself from procrastination as quickly and as easy as possible but not later than three months by using a combination of necessary methods and techniques that would ensure I have*

regained my willpower and killed my identified bad habits from then henceforth so that I can enjoy a healthy and wealthy life richly endowed by loving relationships.

A SMARTEST goal must be;

Specific: a SMART goal must not be ambiguous but specific. A specific goal is that which answers the questions of what (free from procrastination); Why (so that I enjoy a healthy and wealthy live endowed by loving relationships); When (as quickly as possible but, not later than three months); Who (myself); Where (In my mindset) and How (by using a combination of necessary methods and techniques).

Measurable: a SMART goal must be measurable. You must be able to quantify your achievements. In this case, the achievement is killing my *identified habits* (list them) as quickly as possible but not later than three months.

Achievable: a SMART goal must be attainable (achievable). You cannot expect to kill your identified bad habits if you have no willpower. You must work to strengthen your willpower.

Realistic: a SMART goal must be realistic. It must be such that you have both the ability and the will to achieve it. If either will or ability lacks, then, your goal is not realistic. Your will is expressed on how much you are ready to sacrifice to attain your goal. Your ability is what assets (methods, techniques and skills) you have that you can use to execute your will.

Timely: A SMART goal must have a timeframe for its accomplishment. In our example, the timeframe is 'as quickly as possible, but not later than three months'. A goal that is not timely is not a SMART goal for its chances of being achieved cannot be defined.

Empowering: You are not a robot. You are driven not by electricity or fuel but by your inner desire to perform. The greatest drive that boosts your performance is motivation. A motivated person is an inspired person. An inspired person is an empowered person. A goal should be capable of empowering you to strive towards its achievement. To be self-empowered is to ignite your inner inspiration that motivates you to be on a self-drive towards attainment of your set goals and objectives. To achieve this, first and foremost, you must have a transforming vision – a vision which you can easily peep through and see greatness. It must be such a stake that radically boosts your welfare – that makes you much better than you could ever imagine or dream of. In our case, HEALTH, WEALTH AND LOVING RELATIONSHIPS are motivating enough for you to desire to pursue them.

Sensual: A goal must be capable of being felt. It must touch and impact your heart as you think of it. You must be moved by it. You must hold it sentimentally. It must draw in the best of your emotional energy. In our case, ENJOY is such a powerful sensual feeling in our goal. It manifests that feeling of HEALTH, WEALTH and LOVING RELATIONSHIPS.

Transformational: A goal that is transformational is that which radically changes your status of things. One of the greatest causes of your lack of personal development is stagnation accompanied by eventual decay. Stagnation is costly, sometimes much more costly than motion. When there is lack newness and freshness into the way you do things, boredom and monotony sets in. Your rate of default in performance goes high. Your rate of accident also rises due to your state of low levels of alertness. A transformational goal will push you from that stagnant pond of status quo into a new stream of dynamism. In our case, HEALTH, WEALTH and LOVING RELATIONSHIPS are great transformations from the boring, monotonous state of procrastination.

Work on your habit

As we have seen previously, procrastination is a habit. You have to work on your habit so as to change it. The next Section delves into the depth of habit and provides you with a set of DAILY HABITS TO PREVENT PROCRASTINATION.

DAILY HABITS TO OVERCOME PROCRASTINATION

We are always seized by habitual patterns of doing things. Some habitual patterns help us achieve great success while others obstructs us from the same. Thus, we need a deeper understanding of what habits are, which habits we need to keep and which ones we need to discard. This becomes important when it comes to preventing procrastination.

What is a habit?

A habit is a recurrent, (mostly unconscious), pattern of behavior that is achieved through frequent repetition.

How are habits formed?

Habit formation is the way by which a behavior, through repetition, becomes habitual or automatic. The following is a three-step process known as the habit-loop by which habit formation goes through;

1. Trigger
2. Routine

3. Reward

A trigger or cue informs your brain to go into automatic mode and let your behavior unfold. Routine is a sequence of actions regularly followed. Common routines include waking up, going to bathe, taking breakfast and going to school/work. Reward is the positive gain or a like by the brain that makes it remember a particular habit loop.

How a habit stack can help you nurture your daily habits

A habit stack is simply a set of daily habits that you can carry out either in sequence or at a certain given moment or occurrence of an event.

Knowing that procrastination is a habit, it obviously has its own habit loop. Thus, to counter procrastination's habit loop, you use its same trigger but replace the routing and the reward.

Enjoy your freedom from procrastination

Procrastination is some kind of a 'voluntary' prison: A prison where your willpower is enslaved. There is no greater joy that you will experience like that of being free from procrastination; you will wake up early and energized; you will experience vigor in performing your daily tasks; you will feel confident in confronting new challenges; you will witness greater success, prosperity and satisfaction in your life.

Seize the moment. Ride in it. Enjoy it all. There is no turning back.

Yet, to enjoy the eternity of your freedom, you have to engender daily habits as your guards and guarantee against present and future likelihood of procrastination hideously creeping back.

These daily habits include;

1. Mind habits
2. Behavioral habits
3. Lifestyle habits

Mind habits

- Meditate often – Meditation helps to sharpen your focus so that you are able to get to the depth of the root cause of your procrastination.
- Be mindful – Mindfulness helps to boost your self-awareness. Self-awareness is important in determining the root cause of your depleted willpower.
- Engender positivity – Positivity motivates you to take beneficial action against procrastination.
- Be compassionate – Compassion inspires you to snap out of procrastination. It pushes you to overcome inertia and

thus take actions that help to promote greater good for everyone. This is extremely important in caring for your own health and of others; building strong lasting bonds and creating real wealth.

Behavioral habits

- Smile unreservedly – A smile opens your inner being to the warmth of external radiation thus melting the solid ice of inertia within.
- Laugh often and much –Laughing does what a smile does but on a grander scale.
- Take challenge – Every challenge has an opportunity to end procrastination. Every challenge you take is a victory over inertia.
- Embrace defeat wholeheartedly – Fear of losing is one of the greatest motivational forces behind procrastination. Embracing defeat wholeheartedly is not to attach yourself to the perception of loss but to the enjoyment of the game itself.
- Be gracious in your win – Pride always goes for a fall. You cannot win forever. There are times you will lose. Losing is simply parting with the old win so that a new win can become possible. It is not bad in itself but a change that you deserve. When you feel proud to win, you are bound to feel humiliated when you lose. Graciously accepting your

win allows you to lose without humiliation. Humiliation is one of the main fears that make people procrastinate. They fear losing what they already have. Yet, you cannot become productive, and you cannot achieve your best if you fear losing. Losing is not failure but an opportunity for a new chance of winning.

Lifestyle habits

- Eat well – Eating affects your mind. What affects your mind has an effect on your procrastination. Low glycemic diet, lean proteins, nuts, fresh fruits and vegetables, and omega 3 fatty acids are great for your mind as they are great for your brain. Sometimes, procrastination is caused by low brain energy.
- Be active – Carry out chores that allow your body mobility. Exercise often. Play outdoor sports and games. This way, your brain becomes excited and as such, overcoming inertia becomes a reflex action that doesn't necessarily require your conscious input.
- Balance activity – Don't dwell on one activity for long. This is a recipe for monotony and boredom. If an activity ceases to be exciting, switch over to another one. This lowers your inertia and thus helps to avoid procrastination.

- Rest enough – REST! Your body. More so, your brain needs enough time to repair, rebuild and re-energize. Overworking your body and brain will create a natural resistance to new undertakings. If this persists, it becomes habitual which eventually results in procrastination.
- Sleep well – Sleeping is a deliberate part of resting. Yet, it is much more than normal resting. It is a state in which your body is subconsciously taken to a garage. When you fail to sleep enough, your brain becomes foggy. It fails to think fast on the next task to undertake. When it comes to sleep, focus on both quantity and quality. Have proper sleeping habits which include a quiet sleeping environment, respect to your circadian cycle and sufficient dormant time.
- Plan always – Planning, as we have seen, is a great way not to procrastinate. Many people procrastinate simply because there comes a time when nothing triggers them about the next task to do. Having a plan and using simple planning tools such as TO DO List, Diary, Journal, Alarm, etc, helps you to focus in implementing your plan.

How to beat procrastination by changing habits

The following are key steps that you can use to implement your daily habits in order to overcome procrastination;

1. Determine the cue that triggers procrastination

2. Substitute the routine normally triggered by the cue with a positive routine
3. Sublimate negative feedback with a positive one
4. Be self-aware

HOW OVERCOMING PROCRASTINATION WILL IMPROVE YOUR HEALTH, RELATINSHIPS AND MONEY

Overcoming procrastination has immensely unlimited rewards. We simply can't afford to quantify them all in this book. Nonetheless, we can focus on the core areas of our lives where the benefits of overcoming procrastination become immediately and conspicuously apparent.

Health

There are many bad health habits that are necessitated by procrastination which have profound negative effects on your health. Overcoming them greatly boost your health. Some of these negative health habits caused by procrastination are;

- **Delay in seeking medical attention when you feel ill** – Almost all diseases can be cured when early intervention is done. Some of the diseases and/or adverse effects may never be reversed if attended to very late. For example, syphilis, polio, cancer, HIV AIDS, etc are some of the dangerous diseases/conditions which, if not addressed at early onset can have irreversible devastating effects.

- **Delaying going for mobility fitness exercises when you feel signs of numbness and strains** – Numbness, jetlag and such other conditions characterized by sitting or folding your joints for long have been associated with blood clot and even stroke. Arthritis and premature ageing are also associated with lack of physical mobility exercises.
- **Delay brushing your mouth when you detect bad mouth odor** – One of the greatest victims of procrastination is poor dental health. There are many people who, due to procrastination, can hardly brush their teeth after every meal. They can hardly brush their teeth before going to bed. Bad odor is a sign of active bacterial activity in your mouth. This bacterial activity is one which causes plague and tooth decay. Studies too have found out that there is a correlation between persistent bad breathe and heart disease. That means that the negative consequences of bad breathe can affect some other vital body organs.

When you overcome procrastination, you are able to reverse these bad habits and hence;

- **You promptly seek medical attention when you feel ill** – When you seek medical attention on time, you are able to mitigate likely damage from a disease. You are also able to recover as fast as you can. You lose less labor hours or study hours and thus your productivity goes high. You are able to earn more, now and in the future.

- **Stand-up, stretch and take mobility exercises** – Physical mobility helps you to keep off stroke, arthritis and premature ageing, among other painful medical conditions. They also help you to stay younger and live longer. Furthermore, they help to boost your libido and vitality thus making you enjoy your life more and be happier.

- **Save your teeth from decay and have fresh breath** – Teeth are important for eating and digestion. Without teeth, you would hardly eat most of the foods that you are currently eating. Furthermore, teeth help you to have that nice facial form. You can also avoid infections, stomach upsets and even ward off unlikely onset of heart disease by simply keeping your teeth clean. Furthermore, with clean teeth, you can be able to communicate effectively and form lasting bonds.

This shows that procrastination too is a thief of your health.

Relationships

Relationship is one of those areas of one's life that are affected by procrastination. The following are some of the ways by which bad habits of procrastination causes poor or strained relationships;

Delaying gratitude – There are those moments when you felt like saying thanks but procrastination swayed you off. There are those moments you felt like rewarding someone for some good performance but procrastination came to stop it. There are those moments you've felt like embracing someone as an expression of your appreciation but procrastination stole the moment. All these, little by little, steal great opportunity for solid bonds by digging up and expanding fissures in your relationships. Eventually, the relationships become distant and you lose.

Feeling lazy to participate in social activities – Participating in social activities is one of the best ways by which you can expand and strengthen your relationship networks. Unfortunately, procrastination steals away your opportunities; you would have gone for swimming with friends but procrastination tells "that's tiring, you wait for news"; you would have gone visiting friends and relatives but procrastination told "play some video games, they might even come to visit you"; you would have gone to participate in charity events but procrastination told you "there will be a lot of work to do, you aren't strong now"; you would have made a call to congratulate a friend for a great performance, procrastination told you "relax, take a nap and then you will call after". More often than not, those things that we postpone due to procrastination we end up not doing them. Even if we do, due to lateness, their impact is not felt and their desired effect is not as productive.

How overcoming procrastination can boost your relationship:

Impactful gratitude – Without procrastination, you are able to express your gratitude towards others in a timely manner. This helps to boost sincerity of your appreciation as the beneficiaries of your gratitude won't get to feel like it was simply an afterthought and not well-meant.

Productive social participation – Without procrastination, you are able to expand social networks and strengthen bonds. Relationships are simply about participation and communication. The more you communicate and participate on a timely basis, the more productive your relationships become.

As can be seen, procrastination is not just thief of time, but also thief of relationships.

Money

Time is money. Procrastination is the greatest thief of your money.

For us to be able to understand how procrastination not only steals your money but also your wealth, let's dwell deeper into the subject of money and wealth.

Understanding the nature of money

The economists clearly state that money is a measure of value. Lawyers clearly state that money is a legal tender. A tender is simply an offer. Combining both, we can say that money is a legal offer for measuring wealth.

Thus, money offers you a legal means to measure your wealth. It follows that money itself is no wealth but a measure of it – just like a tape measure is not your waist or height but a measure of both.

What is legal depends on the prevailing laws. No countries share the same set of laws. Even in federal jurisdictions such as US, laws vary from State to State. Though, in the US, laws regarding the value of the dollar are relatively uniform. In essence, the value of money depends on the law of a given jurisdiction within which it circulates. Even during the era of primitive States, where batter trade used to be the norm, traders had some sort of unwritten law (agreement) on the exchange value of their goods and services and what was considered as a standard of measure (e.g. gold, silver, bronze, etc).

Money - vs. - Wealth

We have clearly seen that money is not wealth but a measure of it. For money to be a measure of this wealth, this wealth too must be legal. For wealth to be legal, it simply means that it must be recognized as such within a given jurisdiction within which the law applies. Some wealth is considered legal in certain jurisdictions and illegal in others.

Wealth – vs. - Market

Market is simply a space where buyers and sellers meet to transact an exchange of value. This space can be physical or virtual (non-physical). In the era of e-commerce, market is increasingly shifting away from physical space into virtual space.

Not all wealth is marketable. A marketable wealth is a wealth that is recognized by both the buyer and seller as having certain value worth exchange.

Thus, only marketable wealth can be monetized (that is, measured in monetary terms)

The nominal –vs. - real value of money

In economics, there is a big difference between the real and nominal value of money. The legal value of money is always nominal but the real value of money is determined by the value parity between the buyer and seller. This is why the nominal value of $1 is not equal to the nominal value of £1 despite both of them having a denomination of 1.

On the other hand, the real value of either the pound or dollar is determined by the balance between demand pull (or the force with which the buyers are willing pull it to their side and the sacrifice they are willing to give in return) and supply push (or the force with which suppliers are willing to push it away from their side in order to gain the sacrifice that the buyers are willing to give in return).

The time value of money

The worth of money depends on time. Timing is important. This is why a sweater is cheaper in hot season and expensive in cold season. This is because money must be capable of punctually meetings needs of the moment. This is also why, naturally, the value of money depreciates the further you go into the future because, in future, there is no defined need-satisfying demand.

Thus, money obeys time utility – the ability of a product to satisfy consumer's want within a given time.

Knowing, from our previous discussion, that money is not a value but a measure of it, we can say that **money is also a measure of time utility of a given wealth.**

Time utility of wealth is what creates the bulk of wealth in the securities exchange. There is no physical commodity to be exchanged, but time utility of a virtual product. Where is this virtual product? Not in the mind?

What is the right attitude towards money?

The right attitude is to recognize that money is not wealth and while wealth can be monetized, it must be converted into marketable wealth in order for it to be monetized. **Thus, you are not necessarily poor because you not wealthy but, you are simply poor because you have not monetized your wealth – hence, you have no marketable wealth.**

The richest of people in this world are not those who acquired marketable wealth but those who converted their wealth into marketable wealth. In marketing terms, this is known as creating and inducing demand in the mind of the potential buyers. Yes, not all buyers know what they want – sometimes, you have to create and induce a want in them. This is indeed what the bulk of advertisement is all about – creating and inducing a want in the minds of the potential buyers.

So, don't lament that you are poor. Simply find ways to market your wealth, whatever it is, by creating and inducing a want in the minds of potential buyers. This is, in essence, rewiring and/or reprogramming the potential buyers' mindset. But, to achieve this, you must first re-create your mindset – first of all to make it capable of appreciating your power to create wealth. When your mind appreciates this power to create wealth, then, the next logical step is to use the three factors of wealth creation (productivity) to create that need-satisfying wealth. Remember, **the buyer wants to be satisfied, but you need to be satisfied!** So, identify your need, create wealth based on your need, and then, create a want in the buyer's mindset that meets your need represented in the price (the value of your wealth).

So, **money is simply a measure of the market value of the creative power that rests within your mind**. This should be your attitude towards money.

Can procrastination affect the value of money?

As we have seen, is only worth based on;

- Time utility
- Wealth
- Market

Without time utility, money is worthless. For example, if you had money in an auction yard, but you delay making a buy decision and someone else becomes the highest bidder while you could have made a higher bid, you lose the opportunity to own that item. At that moment, your money become worthless in as far as the item you wanted to buy is concerned.

Wealth is created by seizing opportunities. Without seizing opportunities, you cannot create wealth. Without wealth, there is no money! To optimize wealth, you have to boost productivity. Productivity itself is a factor of time. It is a measure of how much of a given quality that you can output within a given time.

Market is a product of time, wealth and relationships. We have seen how procrastination can frustrate and even destroy relationships. We have also seen that to become a successful seller, you have to induce demand in the mind of the buyer. This cannot happen when you cannot create, sustain and promote good relationships. In marketing terms, this relationship is what we commonly refer to as **Customer Care.** With poor customer care, you cannot succeed in the market.

Procrastination steals the market value of your creative power, thus leaving nothing worth being measured by money.

CONCLUSION

Thank you for acquiring this book!

This book "Procrastination: Overcome the bad habits of procrastination and laziness and become more productive" provides hands-on proven practical steps to overcome procrastination.

It is my sincere hope that the information provided in this book has not only enabled you to overcome procrastination but also helped you to regain your productivity. It is also my sincere hope that you have been able help your family, friends and loved ones who are suffering from procrastination to use this book as to set themselves free.

If you are happy about the great information provided in this book, kindly recommend it to others.

Thank you.

Good luck!

The end… almost!

Reviews are not easy to come by.

As an independent author with a tiny marketing budget, I rely on readers, like you, to leave a short review on Amazon.

Even if it's just a sentence or two!

So if you enjoyed the book, please head to the product page, and leave a review as shown below.

I am very appreciative for your review as it truly makes a difference.

Thank you from the bottom of my heart for purchasing this book and reading it to the end.

www.ingramcontent.com/pod-product-compliance
Lightning Source LLC
Chambersburg PA
CBHW071029080526
44587CB00015B/2555